# Weight W Freestyle 2018 Cookbook: Discover Fat & Weight Loss Rapidly (Smart Points Cookbook) 35 Recipes With Photos

## By

## Giorgio James

Copyright 2017. All rights reserved. No part of this publication may be reproduced, stored in a retrieval system or transmitted in any form or by any means, electronic, mechanical, photocopying, recording or otherwise, without prior permission of the publisher.

Limit of Liability / Disclaimer of Warranty: The publisher and author make no representations or warranties with respect or the accuracy or completeness of these contents and disclaim all warranties such as warranties of fitness of a particular purpose. The author or publisher are not liable for any damages whatsoever. The fact that an individual or organization is referred to in this document as a citation or source of information does not imply that the author or publisher endorses the information that the individual or organization provided. This is an unofficial summary & analytical review and has not been approved by the original author of the book.

# Claim Your Free Gift Now

As a way of saying "thank you" for your purchase, we're offering you a free bonus that's *exclusive* for our book readers.

5 Bonus Weight Watchers 2018 Recipes!

Go to the link below before it expires!

http://www.easysummaries.com/wwrecipes

# Weight Watchers Freestyle 2018 Cookbook: Discover Fat & Weight Loss Rapidly (smart points cookbook) 35 recipes with photos

## Contents

Claim Your Free Gift Now

Weight Watchers Freestyle 2018 Cookbook: Discover Fat & Weight Loss Rapidly (smart points cookbook) 35 recipes with photos

   Introduction:

Weight Watchers Freestyle 2018 Major Changes:

Introduction of Weight Watchers Freestyle 2018 New Zero Point Diets:

Weight Watchers Freestyle 2018 Less Daily Points:

Weight Watchers Freestyle 2018 Rollover Points:

Weight Watchers Freestyle 2018 Converting FitPoints to SmartPoints:

Weight Watchers Freestyle 2018 Online Merchandise and Meal Delivery Options:

Weight Watchers Freestyle

2018 FRESHENING BREAKFAST RECIPES

   Berry Oatmeal

   Weight Watchers Freestyle 2018 Recipes

   Sausage Quiche

   Weight Watchers Freestyle 2018 Recipes

Vanilla Crepes

Weight Watchers Freestyle 2018 Recipes

Baked Cherry Pancakes

Weight Watchers Freestyle 2018 Recipes

Mushroom Omelet

Weight Watchers Freestyle 2018 Recipes INNOVATIVE SALADS RECIPES

Tomato & Olive Salad

Weight Watchers Freestyle 2018 Recipes

Arugula Salad

Weight Watchers Freestyle 2018 Recipes

Cucumber & Egg Salad

Weight Watchers Freestyle 2018 Recipes

Kale Salad

Weight Watchers Freestyle 2018 Recipes

Radish & Carrot Salad

Weight Watchers Freestyle 2018 Recipes SIZZLING SOUPS RECIPES

Egg Soup

Weight Watchers Freestyle 2018 Recipes

Beet Soup

Weight Watchers Freestyle 2018 Recipes

Bell Pepper Soup

Weight Watchers Freestyle 2018 Recipes

Carrot & Ginger Soup

Weight Watchers Freestyle 2018 Recipes

Asparagus Soup

Weight Watchers Freestyle 2018 Recipes SAVORY MEAT RECIPES

- Lamb Chops with Tomatoes
- Weight Watchers Freestyle 2018 Recipes
- Spinach Stuffed Chicken Breasts
- Weight Watchers Freestyle 2018 Recipes
- Turkey & Peas
- Weight Watchers Freestyle 2018 Recipes
- Beef & Veggie Casserole
- Weight Watchers Freestyle 2018 Recipes
- Pork Shoulder Roast

Weight Watchers Freestyle 2018 Recipes FINGER LICKING DIPS AND SAUCES

- Spinach Dip
- Weight Watchers Freestyle 2018 Recipes
- Beans Dip
- Weight Watchers Freestyle 2018 Recipes
- Teriyaki Sauce
- Weight Watchers Freestyle 2018 Recipes
- Marinara Sauce
- Weight Watchers Freestyle 2018 Recipes
- Smoky BBQ Sauce

Weight Watchers Freestyle 2018 Recipes SNACKS AND APPETIZERS RECIPES

- Roasted Almonds
- Weight Watchers Freestyle 2018 Recipes
- Spicy Popcorn

Weight Watchers Freestyle 2018 Recipes

    Spinach Chips

    Weight Watchers Freestyle 2018 Recipes

    Cod Sticks

Weight Watchers Freestyle 2018 Recipes BONUS RECIPE

    Cheddar Biscuits

Weight Watchers Freestyle 2018 Recipes Conclusion:

Claim Your Free Gift Now

**FINAL SURPRISE BONUS**

# Weight Watchers Freestyle 2018 Cookbook: Discover Fat & Weight Loss Rapidly (smart points cookbook) 35 recipes with photos

Introduction:

If you are already aware about what really Weight Watcher Program is then it is for sure that you would have heard about the changes they are bringing about in their program for the year 2018. After few years they review and make changes in their program keeping in view modern research and up-to-date scientific developments covering weight loss methodologies. There are a lot of changes to the program and this introduction will cover it all for you.

The program is called Weight Watchers Freestyle in the US and Flex in the United Kingdom.

Prominently, it seems that most of the changes in the program will be towards encouraging people to eat more lean proteins, instead of eating high fat/high sugar foods. This was also evident in the SmartPoints program released in the year 2015. The ability to eat foods like chicken and eggs for zero points will be a very innovative step in the recent program. This is going to be very convenient, it is easy to put together vegetables and lean proteins along a zero point meal. Though these foods are very healthy, yet they have calories and excessive usage of them is going to lead into weight gain. So, a balanced and calculated program is going to make it much easier.

# Weight Watchers Freestyle 2018 Major Changes:

- There will be two hundred Zero Point diets inclusive of foods like fish, eggs, yogurt (fat free), chicken breast and turkey.
- Allocation of fewer daily points.
- Points can be rolled over if they are not in use. Per day addition of points in weekly allowance will be up to 4.
- Introduction of FitPoints which are transferrable to Smart Points.

# Introduction of Weight Watchers Freestyle 2018 New Zero Point Diets:

As in the previous program, the fruits and vegetables are bearing zero points (other than potatoes including both sweet and normal and avocados, which were not zero points in the previous program). The difference is the addition of lean protein having zero point now.

All the recipes which include these foods have to be adjusted by the user to gain the recent SmartPoints value. This is going to be a tough thing for the users.

Following is the list of zero point's addition:

- Yougurt (Fat Free) including Greek.

- Eggs.

- Sea Food like Tilapia, crab, oysters, shrimp and Salmon.

- Cooked & Deli chicken and turkey breast.

- Tofu.

- Tuna canned in spring water.

- Legumes like kidney beans, lentils, chick peas and black beans.

# Weight Watchers Freestyle 2018 Less Daily Points:

You can go to lesser points weekly with the new program. This difference is due to the FREE food they are offering. In case of left daily points value unchanged, the user will be consuming more food and thus will make the program unsuccessful for the user. This will happen due to non-reduction of calorie intake.

# Weight Watchers Freestyle 2018 Rollover Points:

Suppose the allowed limit of daily points is 23 and you are taking only 19. Then these 4 points won't get discarded as in that of the previous programs. These points can now be used in coming allowance and can be used by the user upon his wish. This can be done many times in a sequence in order to save for a big event, but not more than 4 points per day can be rolled over, meaning that there is no starvation allowed.

# Weight Watchers Freestyle 2018 Converting FitPoints to SmartPoints:

This is a confusing portion of the program but not too hard to understand. If a certain fitness goal is achieved, you get FitPoints and then they can be chosen to get them converted into SmartPoints. They can be easily tracked by either using a fitness tracking device or an Apple watch. IF you are unable to do so, they can also be tracked manually.

Before earning a SmartPoint, a walk of 3,000 steps per day is compulsory. Any other exertion of the same value can also be used for this purpose. The very next 1.000 steps or its equitant exertion can earn you a

SmartPoint, which can then be added into your weekly allowed points.

# Weight Watchers Freestyle 2018 Online Merchandise and Meal Delivery Options:

The latest change in the Weight Watchers Freestyle Program 2018 is the option of feed delivery while sitting at your home. This option is alike to the system as offered by other companies like Plated and Blue Apron. This means that there will be planned meals alongside all the required ingredients at your door step. It is reported by many that the meals will be already cooked and a few have stated that the ingredients and recipe of the meal will be sent and you have to cook it personally. This will be depending on the user but will prove to be much convenient in getting points friendly food.

# Weight Watchers Freestyle

# 2018 FRESHENING BREAKFAST RECIPES

## Berry Oatmeal

Serves: 4

Prep Time: 5 mins

Cooking Time: 20 mins

Ingredients:

- 1 cup dry oats
- ½ cup fresh blackberries
- ½ cup fresh cranberries
- ½ cup pecans, chopped
- 1 banana, peeled and mashed
- 4 cups water

**Directions:**

1. Boil oats and water in a large pan over medium-high heat.

2. Reduce the heat to low and simmer for about 15 minutes, occasionally stirring.

3. Remove from heat and keep aside to cool.

4. Stir in mashed banana and top with the berries and pecans to serve.

*Calories* **138**   *Fat* **3.8g**   *Protein* **4.1g**   *Carbohydrates* **23.6g**

**Smart Points:** 5 points

# Weight Watchers Freestyle 2018 Recipes

## Sausage Quiche

**Serves: 4**

**Prep Time: 15 mins**

**Cooking Time: 25 mins**

**Ingredients:**

- 1 cup zucchini, shredded
- ¼ cup Parmesan cheese, shredded
- ¼ cup fat-free milk
- ¼ cup low-fat mozzarella cheese, shredded
- 4-ounce turkey sausages
- 1 red bell pepper, seeded and chopped
- 6 eggs, lightly beaten
- Salt and ground black pepper, to taste

**Directions:**

1. Preheat the oven to 325 degrees F and grease a pie plate.
2. Heat a skillet and add the sausages, zucchini and bell pepper.
3. Cook for about 8 minutes and transfer the sausage mixture into a bowl.
4. Add Parmesan cheese and stir well to combine.
5. Spread the mixture into prepared pie plate evenly.
6. Beat well eggs, milk, salt and black pepper in a medium bowl.
7. Pour egg mixture over the turkey sausage mixture.
8. Sprinkle with mozzarella cheese and bake for about 25 minutes.

*Calories* **179**   *Fat* **9.5g**   *Protein* **16g**

*Carbohydrates* **7.3g**

**Smart Points: 5 points**

# Weight Watchers Freestyle 2018 Recipes

## Vanilla Crepes

**Serves: 2**

**Prep Time: 15 mins**

**Cooking Time: 10 mins**

**Ingredients:**

- 1 tablespoon almond flour
- 2 eggs
- ½ tablespoon olive oil
- 1 tablespoon arrowroot powder
- ¼ teaspoon ground cinnamon
- ½ teaspoon vanilla extract
- Salt, to taste

**Directions:**

1. Add arrowroot powder, almond flour, cinnamon and salt in a bowl.

2. Beat eggs and vanilla in another bowl, until well combined.

3. Combine both the mixtures until well combined.

4. Heat oil over medium heat in a non-stick frying pan.

5. Add desired sized mixture in the pan and tilt the pan to coat the bottom evenly in a thin layer.

6. Cook for about 1 minute on each side and repeat with the remaining mixture.

*Calories* **135**     *Fat* **9.5g**     *Protein* **6.3g**

   *Carbohydrates* **5.5g**

**Smart Points: 4 points**

# Weight Watchers Freestyle 2018 Recipes

## Baked Cherry Pancakes

**Serves: 5**

**Prep Time: 14 mins**

**Cooking Time: 22 mins**

**Ingredients:**

- ½ cup whole-wheat flour
- ½ cup unsweetened almond milk
- 1 teaspoon vanilla extract
- ¼ cup almonds, chopped
- 1 teaspoon olive oil
- 1/8 teaspoon ground cinnamon
- 3 eggs
- 1 tablespoon butter, melted
- 2 cups fresh sweet cherries, pitted and halved

- Pinch of salt

**Directions:**

1. Preheat the oven to 450 degrees F.

2. Add olive oil in an ovenproof skillet, and place the skillet into oven.

3. Mix together flour, cinnamon and salt in a bowl.

4. Add eggs, almond milk, melted butter and vanilla extract and beat until well combined.

5. Add flour mixture into egg mixture and mix until well combined.

6. Take out the skillet from the oven and tilt to spread the oil evenly.

7. Place cherries in the bottom of the skillet in a single layer.

8. Sift the flour mixture over cherries evenly and top with almonds.

9. Bake for about 20 minutes or until an inserted toothpick in the center comes out clean.

10. Remove from oven and allow it to cool for at least 5 minutes before slicing.

11. Cut into equal sized wedges and serve in small plates.

*Calories* **158**   *Fat* **7.8g**   *Protein* **5.8g**   *Carbohydrates* **17.4g**

**Smart Points: 5 points**

# Weight Watchers Freestyle 2018 Recipes

## Mushroom Omelet

**Serves: 3**

**Prep Time: 15 mins**

**Cooking Time: 25 mins**

**Ingredients:**

- ¼ cup unsweetened almond milk
- ¼ cup red bell pepper, seeded and chopped
- 1 tablespoon chives, minced
- 4 large eggs
- ¼ cup onions, chopped
- ¼ cup fresh mushrooms, sliced
- Salt and black pepper, to taste

**Directions:**

1. Preheat the oven to 350 degrees F and grease a pie dish lightly.
2. Add almond milk, eggs, salt and black pepper and beat to mix well.
3. Mix together onions, mushrooms and bell pepper in another bowl.
4. Put the egg mixture in prepared pie dish and top with vegetable mixture evenly.
5. Sprinkle with chives and bake for about 25 minutes.
6. Remove from oven and divide into 4 parts.
7. Top with remaining tomatoes and serve immediately.

*Calories* **107**  *Fat* **7g**  *Protein* **8.9g**

*Carbohydrates* **2.6g**

**Smart Points: 3 points**

# Weight Watchers Freestyle 2018 Recipes
# INNOVATIVE SALADS RECIPES

## Tomato & Olive Salad

**Serves: 10**

**Prep Time: 15 mins**

**Cooking Time: 0 mins**

**Ingredients:**

- 1 (2¼-ounce) can green olives, pitted and chopped
- ¼ cup red wine vinegar
- 5 large tomatoes, chopped
- ½ red onion, sliced thinly
- 5 cucumbers, chopped
- 4-ounce feta cheese, crumbled
- 1 (5-ounce) can black olives, pitted and halved

**Directions:**

1. Mix together all the ingredients except red wine vinegar in a large bowl.

2. Drizzle with red wine vinegar and dish out to serve.

*Calories* **101** *Fat* **5.3g** *Protein* **3.7g** *Carbohydrates* **11.8g**

**Smart Points: 4 points**

# Weight Watchers Freestyle 2018 Recipes

## Arugula Salad

**Serves: 2**

**Prep Time: 12 mins**

**Cooking Time: 0 mins**

**Ingredients:**

- 1/8 cup fresh basil, chopped
- ½ teaspoon garlic clove, minced

- ½ tablespoon olive oil
- ½ tablespoon balsamic vinegar
- Salt and freshly ground black pepper, to taste
- 1 medium ripe tomato, cut into slices
- 1½ cups fresh arugula

**Directions:**

1. Add basil, garlic, olive oil, vinegar, salt and pepper in a small blender and pulse until smooth.

2. Mix together rest of the ingredients in a large serving bowl.

3. Pour dressing and mix to coat well. Serve immediately.

*Calories* 57   *Fat* 4g   *Protein* 2.1g
*Carbohydrates* 4.7g

**Smart Points: 2 points**

# Weight Watchers Freestyle 2018 Recipes

# Cucumber & Egg Salad

**Serves: 4**

**Prep Time: 13 mins**

**Cooking Time: 0 mins**

**Ingredients:**

**For Dressing**

- 2/3 cup fat-free plain Greek yogurt
- 1 garlic clove, minced

- ½ tablespoon Dijon mustard
- Salt and freshly ground black pepper, to taste

**For Salad**

- 2 hard-boiled eggs, peeled and chopped
- 2 medium cucumbers, cut spirally
- ½ cup celery, chopped

**Directions:**

1. Put all the dressing ingredients in a bowl and beat until well mixed.
2. Mix together eggs, cucumber and celery in a large serving bowl.
3. Drizzle the dressing over salad and toss to coat well. Serve immediately.

*Calories* **109**  *Fat* **8.4g**  *Protein* **3.4g**

*Carbohydrates* **12.7g**

**Smart Points: 6 points**

# Weight Watchers Freestyle 2018 Recipes

## Kale Salad

**Serves: 2**

**Prep Time: 15 mins**

**Cooking Time: 5 mins**

**Ingredients:**

- 1 fresh tomato, sliced
- 1 scallion, chopped
- 1 tablespoon fresh lemon juice
- 4 cups fresh kale, trimmed and chopped
- 1 red onion, sliced
- 2 tablespoons fresh orange juice
- 1 tablespoon almonds, chopped

**Directions:**

1. Add all the ingredients except almonds in a large bowl and toss gently to coat well.

2. Cover and refrigerate to marinate for around 8 hours.

3. Remove from the refrigerator and add almonds to serve.

*Calories| 122   Fat| 1.7g   Protein| 5.8g*
*Carbohydrates| 23.3g*

**Smart Points: 4 points**

# Weight Watchers Freestyle 2018 Recipes

## Radish & Carrot Salad

**Serves: 4**

**Prep Time: 12 mins**

**Cooking Time: 0 mins**

**Ingredients:**

**For Salad**

- 3 cups carrots, peeled and julienned
- 1 cup radishes, trimmed, peeled and julienned
- ½ cup fresh parsley, chopped

**For Dressing**

- 2 tablespoons balsamic vinegar
- 2 teaspoons coconut aminos
- ¼ teaspoon garlic, minced
- 1 tablespoon olive oil
- 1 teaspoon fresh ginger, finely grated

- 2 teaspoons raw honey
- Salt, to taste

**Directions:**

1. Mix together all the salad ingredients in a large bowl.

2. Put the dressing ingredients in a small bowl and mix well.

3. Pour the dressing over salad and toss to coat well.

4. Serve immediately in small bowls.

*Calories* 87  *Fat* **3.6g**  *Protein* **1.5g**  *Carbohydrates* **13.1g**

**Smart Points: 4 points**

# Weight Watchers Freestyle 2018 Recipes
# SIZZLING SOUPS RECIPES

## Egg Soup

**Serves: 3**

**Prep Time: 15 mins**

**Cooking Time: 12 mins**

**Ingredients:**

- ½ tablespoon garlic, minced
- 1 egg
- ¼ cup fresh lemon juice
- ½ tablespoon olive oil
- 3 cups chicken broth, divided
- ½ tablespoon arrowroot powder
- Salt and freshly ground white pepper, to taste

**Directions:**

1. Mix together eggs, arrowroot powder, lemon juice, salt, white pepper and 1 cup broth in a bowl.

2. Heat oil over medium-high heat in a large soup pan.

3. Sauté garlic for about 2 minutes and add 2 cups of broth.

4. Bring to boil over high heat and lower the flame.

5. Simmer for about 6 minutes and slowly add egg mixture in the pan.

6. Stir continuously and allow it to simmer for about 5 minutes until desired thickness is achieved.

7. Serve hot in soup bowls.

*Calories* **92** *Fat* **5.3g** *Protein* **7g** *Carbohydrates* **3.2g**

**Smart Points: 3 points**

# Weight Watchers Freestyle 2018 Recipes

## Beet Soup

**Serves: 4**

**Prep Time: 15 mins**

**Cooking Time: 1 hour 30 mins**

**Ingredients:**

- 2 large red beets, trimmed
- 1 tablespoon leek, chopped
- 2 garlic cloves, minced
- 2 bay leaves
- 1/8 teaspoon dried oregano
- 1 tablespoon olive oil
- ½ red onion, chopped
- 2 cups vegetable broth
- 1/8 teaspoon dried basil

- Pinch of dried tarragon
- Pinch of ground cumin
- Pinch of ground cinnamon
- Salt and freshly ground black pepper, to taste

**Directions:**

1. Preheat the oven to 375 degrees F.

2. Wrap the beets in a large piece foil and arrange in a baking sheet.

3. Bake for about 55 minutes and remove from the oven.

4. Allow the beets to cool, peel them and chop them.

5. Heat oil over medium heat in a large soup pan.

6. Sauté onion and leeks for about 5 minutes.

7. Add garlic, bay leaves, herbs and spices and sauté for 2 minutes.

8. Add broth and beets and bring the mixture to a boil.

9. Lower the heat and simmer for about 25 minutes.

10. Discard the bay leaves and allow it to cool slightly.

11. Put soup in batches in a large blender and pulse until smooth.

12. Return the soup into pan over medium heat and stir in salt and black pepper.

13. Cook for about 3 minutes and serve hot.

*Calories* **81** *Fat* **4.3g** *Protein* **3.6g** *Carbohydrates* **7.7g**

**Smart Points: 3 points**

# Weight Watchers Freestyle 2018 Recipes

## Bell Pepper Soup

**Serves: 3**

**Prep Time: 15 mins**

**Cooking Time: 0 mins**

**Ingredients:**

- ½ cup cashews
- ½ cup vegetable broth
- 2 cups red bell pepper, seeded and chopped
- Salt, to taste

**Directions:**

1. Add 1 cup of bell pepper and rest of the ingredients in an immersion blender.

2. Pulse until smooth and transfer the soup into a large bowl.

3. Stir in the remaining bell pepper and serve immediately.

*Calories* **163**   *Fat* **11g**   *Protein* **5.1g**   *Carbohydrates* **13.6g**

**Smart Points: 6 points**

# Weight Watchers Freestyle 2018 Recipes

## Carrot & Ginger Soup

**Serves: 4**

**Prep Time: 15 mins**

**Cooking Time: 30 mins**

**Ingredients:**

- ½ teaspoon vanilla extract

- 1 medium onion chopped

- 1 long red chili, chopped

- 1 tablespoon fresh ginger, peeled and sliced
- 2 cups water
- 3 cups unsweetened almond milk
- 1 tablespoon olive oil
- 2 garlic cloves, minced
- ½ teaspoon fresh turmeric, peeled and sliced
- 4 cups carrots, peeled and chopped
- 2 cups vegetable broth

**Directions:**

1. Heat oil over medium heat in a large soup pan and add onions.

2. Sauté for about 5 minutes and add red chili, garlic and turmeric.

3. Sauté for about 6 minutes and add carrots, water and broth.

4. Boil it and reduce the heat to low.

5. Simmer for about 20 minutes and remove from heat and keep aside to cool slightly.

6. Add soup in batches in a high-speed blender and pulse until smooth.

7. Serve hot in serving bowls.

*Calories* **110**   *Fat* **4.2g**   *Protein* **3.8g**

*Carbohydrates* **15g**

**Smart Points: 5 points**

# Weight Watchers Freestyle 2018 Recipes

## Asparagus Soup

**Serves: 2**

**Prep Time: 15 mins**

**Cooking Time: 10 mins**

**Ingredients:**

- ½ tablespoon olive oil

- 1 scallion, chopped

- ½ pound asparagus, trimmed and chopped
- 2 cups vegetable broth
- 1 tablespoon fresh lemon juice
- Salt and freshly ground black pepper, to taste

**Directions:**

1. Heat oil and scallion over medium heat in a large pan and sauté for about 5 minutes.

2. Add broth and asparagus and bring to boil.

3. Reduce the heat to low and simmer for about 30 minutes.

4. Remove from heat and let it cool slightly.

5. Add soup in batches in an immersion blender and pulse until smooth.

6. Put the soup back into the pan and simmer for about 5 minutes.

7. Stir in the lemon juice, salt and black pepper and remove from heat. Serve hot.

*Calories* **95**   *Fat* **5.1g**   *Protein* **7.5g**   *Carbohydrates* **6g**

**Smart Points: 3 points**

# Weight Watchers Freestyle 2018 Recipes
# SAVORY MEAT RECIPES

## Lamb Chops with Tomatoes

**Serves: 8**

**Prep Time: 18 mins**

**Cooking Time: 7 hours**

**Ingredients:**

- 3 cups tomatoes, chopped finely
- 2 pounds lamb chops
- 1½ cups water
- 6 tablespoons mixed herbs (thyme, oregano, sage)
- Salt and black pepper, to taste

**Directions:**

1. Put all the ingredients in a slow cooker and mix well.

2. Set the slow cooker over low and cook for about 7 hours.

3. Dish out and serve hot.

*Calories* **225** *Fat* **8.5g** *Protein* **32.6g** *Carbohydrates* **3.2g**

**Smart Points: 5 points**

# Weight Watchers Freestyle 2018 Recipes

## Spinach Stuffed Chicken Breasts

**Serves: 4**

**Prep Time: 20 mins**

**Cooking Time: 6 hours 5 mins**

**Ingredients:**

- ½ red pepper, seeded and sliced thinly
- 2 teaspoons fresh lemon juice
- 1 tablespoon olive oil
- 2 teaspoons garlic, minced
- 1 cup chicken broth
- 1 small onion, chopped
- 1 cup fresh spinach, trimmed and chopped
- 4 (4-ounce) skinless, boneless chicken breasts
- 1 pepperoni pepper, seeded and sliced thinly

- ½ teaspoon dried oregano
- Salt and ground black pepper, to taste

**Directions:**

1. Make a deep cut in the middle of one side of each chicken breast with a sharp knife to form a pocket.

2. Heat oil over medium heat in a pan and sauté both peppers and onion for about 2 minutes.

3. Add spinach and garlic and cook for about 3 minutes.

4. Stir in oregano, salt and black pepper and remove from heat.

5. Fill the spinach mixture in each chicken pocket evenly and secure with toothpicks.

6. Transfer the chicken breasts in a slow cooker and stir in lemon juice and broth.

7. Set slow cooker over low and cook for about 6 hours. Serve warm.

*Calories* **183**   *Fat* **5.2g**   *Protein* **28.6g**

*Carbohydrates* **4g**

**Smart Points: 4 points**

# Weight Watchers Freestyle 2018 Recipes

## Turkey & Peas

**Serves: 3**

**Prep Time: 20 mins**

**Cooking Time: 1 hour**

**Ingredients:**

- ½ medium onion, chopped
- 3 garlic cloves, minced
- ¼ teaspoon ground cumin
- ¼ teaspoon ground nutmeg
- ½ pound lean ground turkey
- 1 cup water
- ¼ cup fresh cilantro, chopped
- ¾ cup fresh green peas, shelled
- ¼ cup fresh tomatoes, chopped

- 1 bay leaf
- ¼ teaspoon ground turmeric
- 1 teaspoon ground coriander
- ¼ teaspoon fresh ginger, minced
- ½ tablespoon olive oil
- Salt and freshly ground black pepper, to taste

**Directions:**

1. Put oil and onions in a large pan and sauté for about 4 minutes.

2. Add garlic cloves, ginger and spices and sauté for about 2 minutes.

3. Add turkey and cook for about 6 minutes.

4. Add tomatoes and cook for about 9 minutes.

5. Add water and green peas and cook for about 30 minutes.

6. Stir in salt and black pepper and remove from heat.

7. Garnish with cilantro and serve hot.

*Calories* **175**   *Fat* **8.1g**   *Protein* **17.4g**

*Carbohydrates* **9.1g**

**Smart Points: 5 points**

# Weight Watchers Freestyle 2018 Recipes

## Beef & Veggie Casserole

**Serves: 3**

**Prep Time: 15 mins**

**Cooking Time: 9 hours**

**Ingredients:**

- ½ cup tomatoes, chopped
- ¾ cup fresh green beans
- ½ pound beef steak, cut into thin strips

- ½ medium onion, sliced
- ½ cup fresh mushrooms, sliced
- ¼ cup chicken broth
- Salt and freshly ground black pepper, to taste

**Directions:**

1. Season the beef with the salt and black pepper and put in a slow cooker.

2. Mix in the remaining ingredients and set slow cooker over low.

3. Cook for about 9 hours and serve hot.

*Calories* **167**   *Fat* **5g**   *Protein* **24.7g**

*Carbohydrates* **5.3g**

**Smart Points: 3 points**

# Weight Watchers Freestyle 2018 Recipes

# Pork Shoulder Roast

**Serves: 6**

**Prep Time: 20 mins**

**Cooking Time: 9 hours**

**Ingredients:**

- 2 onions, sliced

- 2 carrots, peeled and sliced

- 2 tablespoons Italian seasonings

- 2 pounds boneless pork shoulder roast
- Salt and freshly ground black pepper, to taste

**Directions:**

1. Mix together pork, Italian seasonings, salt and pepper in a large bowl and keep aside for at least 3 hours.

2. Season the carrots and onions with salt and pepper and place at the bottom of a slow cooker.

3. Transfer the pork over the veggies and set slow cooker over low.

4. Cook for about 9 hours and serve hot.

*Calories* **254** *Fat* **6.7g** *Protein* **40.2g**

*Carbohydrates* **5.9g**

**Smart Points: 5 points**

# Weight Watchers Freestyle 2018 Recipes FINGER LICKING DIPS AND SAUCES

## Spinach Dip

**Serves: 20**

**Prep Time: 20 mins**

**Cooking Time: 35 mins**

**Ingredients:**

- 1 (14-ounce) artichoke hearts, drained and chopped
- ½ cup fat-free sour cream
- 1 (10-ounce) bag frozen chopped spinach, thawed, drained and squeezed
- 2 garlic cloves, minced

- 2 (8-ounce) packages fat-free cream cheese, softened
- ¼ cup low-fat parmesan cheese, grated freshly and divided
- 1 cup part-skim mozzarella cheese, shredded and divided
- Salt and freshly ground black pepper, to taste

**Directions:**

1. Preheat the oven to 350 degrees F.

2. Mix together spinach, artichokes, sour cream, garlic, salt, cream cheese, 1 tablespoon of Parmesan, black pepper and ½ cup of mozzarella cheese in a baking dish.

3. Mix together remaining cheeses in a small bowl and sprinkle the cheese mixture on top of spinach mixture.

4. Bake for about 30 minutes or till bubbly.

5. Preheat the broiler and broil the dip for about 4 minutes. Serve warm.

*Calories* **103**   *Fat* **8.3g**   *Protein* **3.5g**

*Carbohydrates* **4.4g**

**Smart Points: 4 points**

# Weight Watchers Freestyle 2018 Recipes

## Beans Dip

**Serves: 10**

**Prep Time: 20 mins**

**Cooking Time: 35 mins**

**Ingredients:**

- 1 (4-ounce) package low-fat cream cheese, softened
- 1/8 cup scallion, chopped
- 2 drops hot sauce
- ½ cup low-fat sour cream
- 1 (16-ounce) cans refried beans
- 1 tablespoon dried parsley
- ½-ounce package taco seasoning
- 4-ounce low-fat cheddar cheese, shredded
- 4-ounce low-fat Monterrey Jack cheese, shredded

**Directions:**

1. Preheat the oven to 350 degrees F.

2. Add sour cream and cream cheese in a baking dish and mix with fork.

3. Add scallion, beans, hot sauce, parsley, half of cheddar cheese, taco seasoning, half of Monterrey Jack cheese and mix until well combined.

4. Top with remaining cheeses evenly and bake for about 35 minutes. Serve warm.

*Calories* **166**  *Fat* **11.5g**  *Protein* **8.5g**  *Carbohydrates* **7.6g**

**Smart Points: 6 points**

# Weight Watchers Freestyle 2018 Recipes

## Teriyaki Sauce

**Serves: 16**

**Prep Time: 15 mins**

**Cooking Time: 0 minutes**

**Ingredients:**

- 2 garlic cloves, chopped finely
- ¼ cup unsweetened applesauce
- ½ cup coconut aminos
- 2 teaspoons fresh ginger, grated
- ¼ teaspoon red pepper flakes, crushed

**Directions:**

1. Add all ingredients in a bowl and mix until well combined.

2. Transfer the sauce in an airtight glass jar and store in refrigerator for about 6 months.

*Calories* **25**   *Fat* **0g**   *Protein* **0.1g**   *Carbohydrates* **6.2g**

**Smart Points: 1 point**

# Weight Watchers Freestyle 2018 Recipes

## Marinara Sauce

**Serves: 7**

**Prep Time: 20 mins**

**Cooking Time: 30 minutes**

**Ingredients:**

- 1 (14½-ounce) cans stewed tomatoes

- 1/8 cup fresh parsley, chopped

- ½ (6-ounce) can tomato paste
- 1 garlic clove, minced
- ½ teaspoon dried oregano
- ¼ cup olive oil
- ¼ cup white wine
- ¼ cup onion, chopped finely
- Salt and freshly ground black pepper, to taste

**Directions:**

1. Add tomato paste, stewed tomatoes, garlic, parsley and oregano in a food processor and pulse till pulse until smooth.

2. Put oil and onions over medium heat in a large skillet and sauté for about 2 minutes.

3. Add wine and tomato mixture and simmer for about 30 minutes, stirring occasionally.

4. Remove from heat and keep aside to cool before serving.

5. Transfer the sauce in an airtight glass jar and store in refrigerator.

*Calories* 85   *Fat* 7.3g   *Protein* 0.6g   *Carbohydrates* 3.9g

**Smart Points: 3 points**

# Weight Watchers Freestyle 2018 Recipes

## Smoky BBQ Sauce

**Serves: 25**

**Prep Time: 20 mins**

**Cooking Time: 25 minutes**

**Ingredients:**

- 1 cup ketchup
- ¾ cup brown sugar
- 1 tablespoon butter
- ¼ teaspoon celery seeds
- ¼ teaspoon garlic powder
- ¼ teaspoon cayenne pepper
- ¼ teaspoon ground cinnamon
- 1 cup tomato sauce
- ¾ cup red wine vinegar

- ¼ cup molasses
- 2 teaspoons hickory-flavored liquid smoke
- ¼ teaspoon onion powder
- ½ teaspoon paprika
- ¼ teaspoon chili powder
- Salt and freshly ground black pepper, to taste

**Directions:**

1. Mix together all the ingredients in a large pan on medium heat.

2. Reduce the heat to low and simmer for about 25 minutes or until desired thickness.

3. Remove from heat and keep aside to cool before serving.

4. Transfer the sauce in an airtight glass jar and store in refrigerator.

*Calories* **44**   *Fat* **0.5g**   *Protein* **0.3g**

*Carbohydrates* **9.9g**

**Smart Points: 2 points**

# Weight Watchers Freestyle 2018 Recipes SNACKS AND APPETIZERS RECIPES

## Roasted Almonds

Serves: 6

Prep Time: 10 mins

Cooking Time: 15 minutes

### Ingredients:

- 1½ tablespoons unsweetened applesauce
- ½ tablespoon water
- ¼ teaspoon ground cinnamon
- 1/8 teaspoon cayenne pepper
- 1 cup almonds
- ½ teaspoon olive oil
- ¼ teaspoon red chili powder
- 1/8 teaspoon ground cumin
- Salt, to taste

### Directions:

1. Preheat the oven to 350 degrees F.
2. Arrange the almonds onto a baking sheet in a single layer and roast for about 10 minutes.
3. Add applesauce and microwave over high for about 45 seconds in a microwave safe bowl.

4. Remove from microwave and add oil and water.

5. Mix together all the spices in a small bowl and remove the almonds from oven.

6. Add almonds into the bowl of applesauce mixture and stir to combine well.

7. Transfer the almond mixture onto baking sheet in a single layer and sprinkle with spice mixture evenly.

8. Roast for about 4 minutes and remove from oven and keep aside to cool completely before serving.

*Calories|* **102**   *Fat|* **8.4g**   *Protein|* **3.4g**

   *Carbohydrates|* **5.2g**

**Smart Points: 3 points**

# Weight Watchers Freestyle 2018 Recipes

## Spicy Popcorn

**Serves: 3**

**Prep Time: 15 mins**

**Cooking Time: 5 minutes**

**Ingredients:**

- ½ cup popping corn
- ¼ teaspoon garlic powder
- 3 tablespoons olive oil, divided
- 1 teaspoon ground turmeric
- Salt, to taste

**Directions:**

1. Heat 2 tablespoons of oil over medium-high heat in a pan.

2. Add popping corn and cover the pan tightly.

3. Cook for about 2 minutes, shaking the pan occasionally or until corn kernels start to pop.

4. Remove from heat and transfer into a large heatproof bowl.

5. Stir in remaining olive oil and spices and serve immediately.

*Calories* | **183**   *Fat* | **2g**   *Protein* | **1.8g**   *Carbohydrates* | **12.6g**

**Smart Points: 6 points**

# Weight Watchers Freestyle 2018 Recipes

## Spinach Chips

**Serves: 4**

**Prep Time: 20 mins**

**Cooking Time: 10 minutes**

**Ingredients:**

- ¼ teaspoon olive oil
- ¼ teaspoon ground cumin
- 8 cups fresh spinach leaves
- ½ teaspoon paprika
- Salt, to taste

**Directions:**

1. Preheat the oven to 325 degrees F and line a baking sheet with a parchment paper.

2. Put spinach leaves in a large bowl and drizzle with oil.

3. Rub the spinach leaves gently with oil and sprinkle with spices and salt.

4. Transfer the leaves onto prepared baking sheet in a single layer.

5. Bake for about 10 minutes and serve immediately.

*Calories*| 18    *Fat*|0.6g    *Protein*|1.8g
*Carbohydrates*| 2.4g

**Smart Points: 1 points**

# Weight Watchers Freestyle 2018 Recipes

## Cod Sticks

**Serves: 8**

**Prep Time: 20 mins**

**Cooking Time: 15 minutes**

**Ingredients:**

- 1 cup almond flour
- ½ teaspoon cayenne pepper
- 1 cod fillet, sliced thinly
- 2 eggs
- 2 teaspoons dried parsley, crushed
- Salt and freshly ground black pepper, to taste

**Directions:**

1. Preheat the oven to 350 degrees F and grease a large baking sheet lightly.

2. Beat the eggs in a bowl and mix together parsley, cayenne pepper, flour, salt and black pepper in another bowl.

3. Dip the cod sticks in egg and then coat with flour mixture.

4. Arrange the cod strips into prepared baking sheet in a single layer.

5. Bake for about 12 minutes, flipping once in the middle way and serve warm.

*Calories|* **111**     *Fat|* **7.9g**   *Protein|* **6.9g**

   *Carbohydrates|* **3.2g**

**Smart Points: 3 points**

# Weight Watchers Freestyle 2018 Recipes
# BONUS RECIPE

## Cheddar Biscuits

**Serves: 8**

**Prep Time: 20 mins**

**Cooking Time: 15 minutes**

**Ingredients:**

- ¼ teaspoon baking powder
- 1/8 teaspoon ginger powder
- ¼ cup butter, melted and cooled
- 1/3 cup coconut flour, sifted
- 1/8 teaspoon garlic powder
- 4 eggs
- 1 cup low-fat sharp cheddar cheese, shredded

**Directions:**

1. Preheat the oven to 400 degrees F and line a large cookie sheet with greased foil paper.
2. Mix together flour, baking powder, garlic powder and salt in a large bowl.
3. Add eggs and butter in another bowl and beat well. Add flour mixture into egg mixture and beat until well combined.
4. Stir in cheese and place the mixture onto prepared cookie sheets in a single layer.
5. Bake for about 15 minutes until top becomes golden brown.

*Calories|* **142**   *Fat|* **12.7g**   *Protein|* **6.4g**

*Carbohydrates|* **0.8g**

**Smart Points: 6 points**

# Weight Watchers Freestyle 2018 Recipes Conclusion:

It is really hard to beat Weight Watchers in any healthy weight loss program for a long term. Whether it is named Flex or Freestyle, the introduction of proteins in zero points is very catchy. The reason is that medical science has proven that consumption of proteins is very necessary to remain healthy. This innovation is going to make the program user friendly and convenient. The inclusion of lean proteins as Zero Point Diets will make the program much easier for the participants. You can also reallocate your daily points in coming days if they aren't used previously. With the advent of new ZeroPoint diets, the program has become catchier for the participants. This newly released program has almost every possible easily adaptable habits and diet plans to let you maintain or lose weight. The emphasis laid on exercise and 5k is appreciative in the app. The integration of fitness tracking devices in the 2018 Weight Watchers Program is also the reason for its popularity. The Weight Watchers has also launched a delivery system for its customers, so that you can have your diet plan right at your door step and help you in living a healthy fat free life.

# Claim Your Free Gift Now

As a way of saying "thank you" for your purchase, we're offering you a free special bonus that's *exclusive* for our book readers.

5 Bonus Weight Watchers 2018 Recipes!

## Go to the link below before it expires!

http://www.easysummaries.com/wwrecipes

# FINAL SURPRISE BONUS

Final words from the author…

Hope you enjoyed this book as much as we enjoyed bringing it to you!

I always like to over-deliver, so I'd like to give you one final bonus.

**Do me a favor, if you enjoyed this book, please leave a review.**

It will help get the word out so more readers can enjoy this book!

If you do, I'll send you one of my most cherished collection – Free:

**5 More Tantalizing Recipes on Weight Watchers Freestyle 2018 Cookbook: Discover Fat & Weight Loss Rapidly (smart points cookbook) 35 recipes with photos and Giorgio James!**

Here's how to claim your free report:

1. Leave a review (longer the better but I'd be grateful for whatever length)

2. Send your email address here:
easysummaries24@gmail.com

Receive your free bonus – 5 More Tantalizing Recipes on Weight Watchers Freestyle 2018 Cookbook: Discover Fat & Weight Loss Rapidly (smart points cookbook) 35 recipes with photos and Giorgio James! – *immediately*!